THE PEARL HARBOR STORY

AUTHENTIC INFORMATION AND PICTURES OF THE ATTACK ON PEARL HARBOR DECEMBER 7, 1941

by CAPTAIN WILLIAM T. RICE, USNR (Ret)

© Copyright Tongg Publishing Company 1991
Published and Printed by Tongg Publishing Company
P.O. Box 2113, Honolulu, Hawaii, U.S.A.
Twenty-fifth printing 1994

JAPANESE CARRIER

Crewmen cheer as wave after wave of planes are launched for the attack. 353 planes took off from the flight decks of 6 Japanese carriers on the morning of December 7, 1941; 183 at 6:00 a.m. and a second wave of 170 followed at 7:15. Pearl Harbor was the objective of their lethal attack.

The carriers were in a 33 ship task force which had crept without detection to 200 miles north of Oahu.

As the planes approached the island they split into three groups. Some dove on Pearl Harbor from the west, strafing the Marine Airfield at Ewa, others from the north hitting Schofield Barracks and Wheeler Field as they came in low towards their main target, and the rest zoomed in from the east past Diamond Head.

At 5 minutes to 8:00 o'clock they converged on Pearl Harbor and by 1:00 p.m. all but 29 were back aboard their carriers.

The Task Force immediately left the area on a direct route to Japan. Before the end of the war every one of the 33 ship force, with the exception of one destroyer, had been sunk.

2

JAPANESE ATTACK FORCE

SIX CARRIERS
Akagi
Kaga
Hiryu
Soryu
Shokaku
Zuikaku

2 BATTLESHIPS
2 HEAVY CRUISERS
1 LIGHT CRUISER
9 DESTROYERS
3 SUBMARINES ("I" Type)

KURILE IS.

RENDEZVOUS NOV. 22

DEC. 3

HOKKAIDO

TOKYO

MARCUS

IWO JIMA

PLANES RECOVERED

MIDWAY

LAUNCHING POINT
0600 DEC. 7

WAKE ATTACHED DEC. 8
SURRENDERED DEC. 23

KAUAI

OAHU   HAWAII

**ROUTES
OF ATTACKING PLANES
7 DECEMBER 1941**

Kahuku

Haleiwa Field

Mokuleia Field

Kaena Pt.

Schofield

Wheeler Field

Kaneohe
Bay

MCAS

PEARL HARBOR

Bellows
Field

MCAS

Hickam Field

HONOLULU   Makapuu Pt.

Barbers Pt.

Diamond Head

OAHU

USS CONDOR

USS CONDOR was on routine mine-sweeping patrol duty offshore the island of Oahu in the early morning of December 7, 1941.

At about 3:45 a.m. men of her crew spotted a submarine in the restricted waters near the entrance to Pearl Harbor. CONDOR's skipper signalled to the Destroyer WARD, which was also on patrol nearby, giving the CONDOR's position and reporting what they had seen.

As the CONDOR was only equipped for mine-sweeping, and the WARD was armed with guns and depth charges, CONDOR left the area and proceeded into Pearl Harbor, her patrol duty time being completed.

The anti-submarine nets in the channel had been opened for the CONDOR since she was scheduled to come in at that hour.

USS WARD

USS WARD responded to the message from the CONDOR by speeding to the area but could not locate the submarine. Both the CONDOR and the WARD considered the idea that one of our own submarines might be in the restricted area by error. Nevertheless the WARD went to battle stations but found nothing.

In the daylight, at about 7:00 a.m., the WARD sighted a submarine and again went to action stations. They sank the midget Japanese submarine near the Pearl Harbor Channel entrance and the commanding officer of the

WARD sent this terse message to the commandant of the 14th Naval District in Pearl Harbor:

"We have attacked, fired upon, and dropped depth charges upon a submarine operating in defensive sea area."

Neither the text nor the implications of this message were distributed to the fleet in time to warn them of the impending enemy attack.

The destroyer WARD is officially recognized for having fired the first shot of World War II.

Three years later to the day, December 7, 1944, the WARD was sunk at Ormac Bay in the Philippines after a Kamikaze suicide plane crashed on her.

MIDGET JAPANESE SUBMARINES,

transported from Japan to Hawaii on the top of large Japanese "I" class subs, took part in the December 7, 1941 attack. The midgets, designed in Germany and built in Japan, varied between 40 and 50 feet in length and accommodated a two man crew. They could fire two torpedoes and were also equipped with an explosive charge in the bow for suicidal ramming. One sub couldn't steer properly and finally beached on the Windward side of Oahu. The skipper was the first Japanese prisoner-of-war. All other crews were killed in their vessels.

One sub penetrated Pearl Harbor through the open submarine nets an hour or so before the air attack, but did no damage. It was sunk when the destroyer MONAGHAN rammed the midget vessel.

Two subs were sunk just outside Pearl Harbor: one by the WARD just before 7:00 a.m. and the other by the light cruiser ST. LOUIS at about 9:45 a.m.

TWELVE B-17 BOMBERS

from California arrived over Oahu during the December 7th air raid on Pearl Harbor. They had been disarmed to lighten their loads. In one, Staff Sergeant Lee Embree opened a hatch as Zeros approached, swung out his large aerial camera and recorded the only U.S. aerial pictures of the attack. Enemy pilots apparently thought the camera was a gun and avoided the plane. (This picture taken over the wing of the B-17 shows "Val" dive bombers.)

The other bombers were attacked, but all managed to land: eight at Hickam Field, two at Haleiwa Field, one at Bellows Field, and one on the Kahuku Golf Course.

At Point Kahuku an Army radar operator picked up the Japanese mass of planes about 7:00 a.m. He reported this to his headquarters but the B-17 flight had been widely publicized and it was assumed they were responsible for the radar detection. Had the approaching planes been considered as non-friendly, there could have been an alert 50 minutes before the attack.

hickAM ARMY AIRfield

was busy with more than the usual Sunday activities early that day of December 7th as many officers and men were on hand for the arrival of the B-17 flight from California. The Japanese arrived first, bombing and strafing Hickam Field at the same moment they hit Pearl Harbor.

The attack was relentless and set fire to barracks, hangars and planes. The Army bombers that were grouped together along the runway as an anti-sabotage measure were quickly put out of action. Japanese destruction was thorough; smouldering wreckage littered the base, and Hickam Field was out of the fight for that day.

Wheeler Field, 12 miles away, was also bombed and strafed but managed to get some fighter planes up. Other planes took off from Haleiwa Field which was not attacked.

Oahu was home base for about 390 military planes; only 38 were able to get airborne; 10 of them were shot down.

PEARL HARBOR

PEARL HARBOR has 8.5 square miles of water area and there are about 12 miles of docking facilities. The main body of water is joined by smaller areas called lochs and bays.

The present development of the harbor occurred in various stages. In 1902 the channel was dredged to a depth of 35 feet but it wasn't until 1908 that the facilities inside were expanded, as they were again in 1919, 1922 and a great deal more about 1941.

Ford Island is in the center of the main body of water and was the site of the Naval Air Station on December 7th. Both sides of Ford Island were lined with mooring quays, the ones on the south-east side comprising a group known as "Battleship Row." At that time, quays were used exclusively by the largest ships because it was difficult to moor them in the smaller docking areas.

PEARL HARBOR CHANNEL had been protected since 1909 by Fort Kamehameha named after the great Hawaiian warrior and king. That Coast Artillery fort and later Fort Weaver and Fort Barrette bracketed both sides of the channel with 12 inch mortars and 16 inch naval guns converted to coast artillery use.

That defense was of no protection during the air attack on December 7, 1941. The guns were melted down for scrap in the early days of the war.

The channel's only other defense was, the two submarine nets that were stretched across at different points. The defense proved vulnerable when a midget sub followed our ships into the harbor while the nets were open.

During the war Fort Kamehameha was used as a clearance center with many thousands of men leaving there for battle areas and later for many returning for furloughs, rotation and discharge. The Forts are no longer active.

PEARL CITY PENINSULA

PAN AMERICAN CLIPPER BASE

MEDUSA

CURTISS

MIDDLE LOCH

WAIPIO PENINSULA

WEST LOCH

PEARL HARBOR
7 DECEMBER 1941

PEARL HARBOR NAVAL HOSPITAL

was a small facility on the morning of December 7, 1941. In the course of the ferocious assault, there was a recorded total of 3,478 casualties in the area near the hospital. More than 2,000 wounded needed first aid, medical care or hospitalization. Teams of doctors, nurses and aides worked at the Naval Hospital 24 hours a day for 10 days following the attack.

Not only was the Naval Hospital over-burdened but the hospitals throughout the city of Honolulu were filled to overflowing. Four school buildings were converted into temporary hospitals to care for the injured.

Civilian help from doctors, nurses, civilian defense teams, blood banks and blood donors were immediately available because of a well organized Civilian Defense program. The project had been initiated and well developed in the months prior to the attack and saved many lives.

USS NEVADA

USS NEVADA was the only battleship to get underway during the air attack on December 7, 1941. One Japanese torpedo hit in the forward section but even with that damage the crew hastily cut her lines as she left the mooring quays. The intention of the commanding officer was to put to sea as ordered. Enemy attack planes diverted from other targets and dive-bombed the fleeing vessel.

As the NEVADA passed abeam of the southwestern point of Ford Island the water around the ship erupted in huge geysers from the devastating deluge of bombs. She emerged from the spray with her superstructure on fire and her hull a series of gaping holes but she was still underway. However, the NEVADA did not escape. She was ordered to deliberately run aground to avoid the risk of sinking and blocking the channel, thus imprisoning the other ships.

In the shallow water on a hard sand bottom of what is now called Nevada Point, repairs and salvage work went rapidly and the NEVADA survived to fight again.

FORD ISLAND NAVAL AIR STATION

and Hickam Field were bombed and strafed simultaneously on December 7, 1941. To prevent counter attacks the Japanese hit the air bases on the island first. The Naval Air Station at Kaneohe, Wheeler and Bellows Army Air Fields and the Marine Air base at Ewa were all attacked at nearly the same time, virtually eliminating the island's air capabilities.

Because of the war in Europe the United States had become extremely sabotage conscious and directives had gone to all branches of the Armed Services to take precautions against possible sabotage. In carrying out those orders planes were taken from hangers and placed in groups along runways. Being out in the open, the planes were more easily guarded.

The conveniently grouped planes made easy targets for attacking enemy pilots and Ford Island was left with only three operable aircraft. Unable to counter-attack by air, the men rushed to set up machine guns, firing at the dive bombers from the ground. At every base men were courageously retaliating with whatever weapons were left to them.

USS CURTISS

(lower left) sounded General Quarters at 7:55 a.m. just after Ford Island was hit by the first bomb on December 7, 1941. She commenced firing at attacking aircraft and prepared to get underway. At 8:06 a.m. the firing was diverted to an enemy sub off her starboard quarter, continuing until the destroyer MONAGHAN steamed down on the sub.

The CURTISS shot down three planes that morning but unluckily one of them crashed into the ship setting her afire and she was trapped at her moorings.

Along the northwest side of Ford Island (right to left) are the TANGIER, UTAH, RALEIGH and DETROIT.

The TANGIER's anti-aircraft firing started at 8:00 a.m. Just after that time its bow guns were fired at the midget sub, but like the CURTISS ceased firing as the MONAGHAN approached. Four bombs narrowly missed the TANGIER which escaped the attack undamaged.

The picture shown was taken by an attacking Japanese pilot before 8:00. The UTAH had already been hit.

USS MONAGHAN

USS MONAGHAN was a ready duty destroyer on the morning of December 7, 1941. At 7:51 a.m. she was ordered to get underway immediately and join the destroyer WARD off the entrance to Pearl Harbor. Moving out of East Loch she passed between the CURTISS and the TANGIER as both were firing at the midget sub which had surfaced.

The MONAGHAN put on flank speed, rammed the sub and dropped two depth charges as her bow glanced off it. That ended the brief career of the sub. The MONAGHAN proceeded out of the harbor to join other ships in the search for the Japanese fleet.

The MONAGHAN earned 12 battle stars and survived many engagements without serious damage. On December 17, 1944, the MONAGHAN capsized in a typhoon near the Philippines. The storm with winds of 110 knots accomplished what the enemy had been unable to do. Only six men of the entire crew survived.

USS UTAH

was one of the first ships hit that Sunday of December 7th. She took two torpedoes within five minutes of the beginning of the attack and listed so rapidly the senior officer aboard ordered "abandon ship." No one had finished hoisting the flag that was to be raised at 8:00 a.m. By 8:12 the UTAH was bottom up, a total loss. Four hundred sixty-one men survived the sinking of the UTAH. Fifty-eight perished in the strafing attacks, or were trapped inside the ship. One man was saved by cutting through the up-turned bottom.

The UTAH was built as Battleship #31 and during World War I was a Flagship in the Atlantic. In 1931 she was converted to a mobile target vessel with her heavy guns removed and decks of heavy timbers and cement constructed as protection against the practice bombs dropped on her. From 1935 on, UTAH was also designated and staffed as an anti-aircraft training ship but she did not have time to use these powerful batteries that morning.

She was declared "out of commission" in 1944 when salvage work was abandoned. Being moored in "Aircraft Carrier Row" made her a prime target for the early, fierce attack, and it's possible her heavy, protective decks led enemy pilots to mistake the UTAH for a carrier.

JOHN VAESSEN was working at his switchboard when the explosions rocked the UTAH. He could feel the ship listing to port as the order was given to abandon ship. Vaessen stayed at his post and later said, "I was very busy flipping switches trying to keep lighting at least."

He was trapped in the overturned hull. Hammering and hammering on the hull, he finally heard sounds outside. At last he saw daylight and inhaled fresh air.

Bill Hill, a Shipfitter from the RALEIGH, helped Vaessen through the hole he had cut and told him what was happening.

THE SECRETARY OF THE NAVY
WASHINGTON
The President of the United States takes pleasure in presenting the
NAVY CROSS to
JOHN B. VAESSEN, FIREMAN SECOND CLASS, U.S. NAVAL RESERVE for service as set forth in the following CITATION:
"For distinguished service in the line of his profession, extraordinary courage and disregard of his own safety during the attack on the Fleet in Pearl Harbor, Territory of Hawaii, by Japanese forces on December 7, 1941. Although realizing that the ship was capsizing and having been ordered to abandon ship, Fireman Vaessen remained at his post at the forward distribution board of the U.S.S. UTAH and kept lights burning as long as possible, later being rescued through a hole cut in the bottom of the ship.

For the President,
Frank Knox,
Secretary of the Navy

18

USS UTAh And MEMORIAL

"NEAR THIS SPOT AT BERTH FOX 11, ON THE MORNING OF 7 DECEMBER 1941, THE USS UTAH WAS STRUCK ON THE PORTSIDE WITH WHAT IS BELIEVED TO HAVE BEEN THREE AERIAL TORPEDOS AND WAS SUNK. SHE WAS SUBSEQUENTLY ROLLED OVER TO CLEAR THE CHANNEL BUT WAS LEFT ON THE BOTTOM." (Inscription from USS Utah Memorial plaque)

USS RALEIGH

USS RALEIGH was moored just ahead of the UTAH on the northwest side of Ford Island on December 7, 1941. (The capsized UTAH is in the background.)

In the first wave of attackers a torpedo hit the RALEIGH on the port side causing a list to such a degree that it appeared she might capsize. Within minutes of the attack her anti-aircraft batteries were firing but the attack of a dive bomber was unavoidable. The ship was strafed and the deck hit with an armor-piercing shell that went through the ship and exploded in the mud beneath her. As she fought to survive, the gunners assisted in the destruction of five planes, blowing the tail off one as it passed astern. By some miracle not one man was killed and only a few wounded.

The other part of the fight was to keep afloat. In this action, the RALEIGH succeeded, was soon repaired, and then went on to fight the enemy.

USS dETROiT

USS DETROIT was moored just ahead of her sister cruiser the RALEIGH when Pearl Harbor was attacked, December 7th.

The same wave of torpedo planes that hit the RALEIGH and the UTAH sent one torpedo at the DETROIT which skimmed by her and detonated against Ford Island. The DETROIT gun crews got in some hits on enemy planes. However, she was so close to the RALEIGH, and with both ships firing at will, it was difficult to determine which guns scored.

The DETROIT was not damaged during the attack. She joined two other cruisers, ST LOUIS and PHOENIX, the destroyers WARD, HELM, MONAGHAN, BLUE, TUCKER, BAGLEY, DALE HENLEY, PHELPS, and other ships in the fruitless search for the Japanese forces.

The DETROIT earned six battle stars. After Pearl Harbor she participated in the Aleutian patrols and occupation of Attu, the attacks on the Kurile Islands, the Iwo Jima and Okinawa assaults and occupations, and the Third Fleet operations against Japan.

USS SOLACE

a hospital ship, was moored in East Loch the morning of December 7, 1941. Her status as a hospital ship was plainly evident: hull painted white, large red crosses on both sides and topside. Japanese flyers did not bomb the SOLACE.

That was fortunate because of the limited facilities at the Pearl Harbor Naval Hospital and hospitals throughout the city. The medical supplies,

equipment and personnel aboard the SOLACE were badly needed.

Launches from the SOLACE were out in the middle of the attack picking up wounded men from the flaming water and returning with them for treatment as fiery explosions blasted on every side. The non-medical crew from the SOLACE helped at other ships saving men and equipment.

Moored in East Loch near the SOLACE were destroyer tenders with their groups of destroyers. Some of them went out of the harbor during the attack, and others soon afterward, to join in the hunt for the attacking forces.

THE FIRST MINUTES OF WAR

are shown in the captured Japanese aerial photograph taken December 7, 1941.

"Battleship Row" along the east side of Ford Island had received its first torpedoes. Two Japanese planes are in view, one over the NEOSHO and one over Southeast Loch.

The fuel tanks (shown in the background) at the Navy's fuel oil storage depot went untouched during the attack. So did the Submarine Base of Southeast Loch (upper right). Early retaliation against the infamous attack was possible to a great degree because these facilities escaped damage. The five submarines in the Sub Base during the attack were able to start harrassing the Japanese in the Western Pacific within a few days and plenty of fuel was available for all ships.

"BATTLESHIP ROW"

just after the first torpedoes hit shows the explosions making concentric waves in the water. Oil slicks can be seen close alongside the WEST VIRGINIA, OKLAHOMA and CALIFORNIA. More than 2,000 men were killed here in the first 30 minutes of the December 7, 1941 attack.

From left to right are the battleships NEVADA, VESTAL (a repair ship), ARIZONA (inboard), WEST VIRGINIA (outboard), TENNESSEE (inboard), OKLAHOMA (outboard), MARYLAND (inboard), NEOSHO (a tanker) and CALIFORNIA.

The first and very disastrous blows were by 12 torpedo planes that made a low approach from the east over Southeast Loch. Salvaged torpedoes showed that specially contrived wooden fins were fitted to them so they could be launched in shallow water. None of the ships had torpedo nets rigged because they were confident the shallow water protected them against torpedoes.

Smoke, in the background, is from the fires started at Hickam Army Air Field following the bombing and strafing of the hangars, planes, and buildings.

USS NEVADA

participated in both global wars in the first half of the Twentieth Century. The first oil-burning battleship in the U.S. Navy, the NEVADA was the oldest United States battleship afloat on December 7th. During that attack she was ordered aground. Later the ship was raised from the mud, refloated and repaired at Pearl Harbor, and then completely modernized at Bremerton Shipyards.

After a short time in the Aleutians she hurriedly sailed through the Panama Canal to join in the invasion of France, both on the Normandy Coast and on the Southern Coast. Then she was back in the Pacific for the Iwo Jima, Okinawa and Japan occupations. The NEVADA served her country as a "guinea pig" for the Bikini Atom bomb tests in 1946. Surviving the atom tests she was sunk in 1948 by American ships while testing other weapons.

USS ARIZONA

USS ARIZONA was placed in commission in 1916. For 25 years the U.S. Navy, the people of the state for which she was named and other U.S. citizens were proud of the ARIZONA. The mighty dreadnaught of the high seas was prepared to meet any enemy.

The battleship ARIZONA was the third U.S. ship to bear the name. The first ARIZONA was an ironclad side-wheel steamer purchased by the Government in 1863. The second ARIZONA was a frigate launched in 1865. There will be no others named ARIZONA.

The over-all length of the ARIZONA was 608 feet, her beam 97 feet. Her normal displacement was 31,400 tons with a mean draft of 29 feet.

Of her total complement of Navy and Marine Corps men, some 1,550 were on board that fateful morning.

U.S.S. ARIZONA

THUNDERING EXPLOSIONS

jolted the mighty ARIZONA as five torpedoes ripped into her portside. In addition, an uncounted number of aerial bombs hit her decks. An armor-piercing shell penetrated the upper decks and continued down into the forward powder magazine. The explosion that followed knocked out all electrical circuits and all communications. Concussion of the explosion set off the ARIZONA's main forward battery magazine which lay deep in the vessel's hull below gun turrets No. 1 and No. 2. The combined weight of the two turrets was more than 600 tons, including their heavy armor plating and their triple 14 inch guns, yet the force of that tremendous explosion was so great it dislodged both of the gun turrets and the conning tower and they all dropped vertically about 20 feet below their normal positions.

The proud ARIZONA went down in the greatest assault ever made on the United States, the treacherous Japanese attack on Pearl Harbor. After many years of service with the fleet in the Pacific her end came with sudden and enveloping destruction and death on December 7, 1941.

THE ARIZONA was shattered in two and settled to the bottom of the harbor in less than nine minutes. Oil in parts of the hull and on the water burned as a holocaust for hours. The ARIZONA defiantly continued to fly her flag which was hoisted as the attack began.

Only 289 persons survived the terrible explosions and fires. Four-fifths of the ship's complement of men were killed, by far the heaviest personnel loss of all the ships in the harbor.

The bodies of more than 1,100 men are still entombed within the rusting hulk, among them Rear Admiral Isaac C. Kidd and Captain Franklin Van Valkenburgh, commanding officer of the ARIZONA.

It was decided to allow the ARIZONA to rest in her underwater grave as a nautical tomb in memory of the men who made the ultimate sacrifice for their country on December 7, 1941.

USS ARIZONA MEMORIAL

In 1957 a fund-raising campaign was started to raise $500,000 for a permanent memorial. The following year Congress authorized the proposed building as a national shrine.

Through the help of individuals and businesses, newspaper editors nationwide, the television show *This is your Life* and a benefit performance by Elvis Presley, most of the money was raised. The U.S. Congress then added $150,000 and the State of Hawaii $50,000.

The memorial was dedicated in a solemn ceremony on Memorial Day 1962. It spans the sunken hull of the ARIZONA where the bodies of more than 1,100 men are still entombed.

Within the Memorial is a museum, a shrine where the names of the ARIZONA crewmen who died are inscribed on a marble wall and an assembly area large enough to accommodate two hundred people where memorial services are held.

In 1950 Admiral Arthur W. Radford ordered the flag to be flown at the top of the mast and the ARIZONA has since then been considered sentimentally in commission. Every morning and evening a color guard raises and lowers the flag.

The inscription on a bronze plaque at the foot of the flagpole reads:

DEDICATED
TO THE ETERNAL MEMORY
OF OUR GALLANT SHIPMATES
IN THE USS ARIZONA
WHO GAVE THEIR LIVES IN ACTION
7 DECEMBER 1941
"From today on the USS ARIZONA will again fly our country's flag just as proudly as she did on the morning of 7 December 1941.
I am sure the ARIZONA's crew will know and appreciate what we are doing." Admiral A. W. Radford. USN
7 March 1950
MAY GOD MAKE HIS FACE
TO SHINE UPON THEM
AND GRANT THEM PEACE

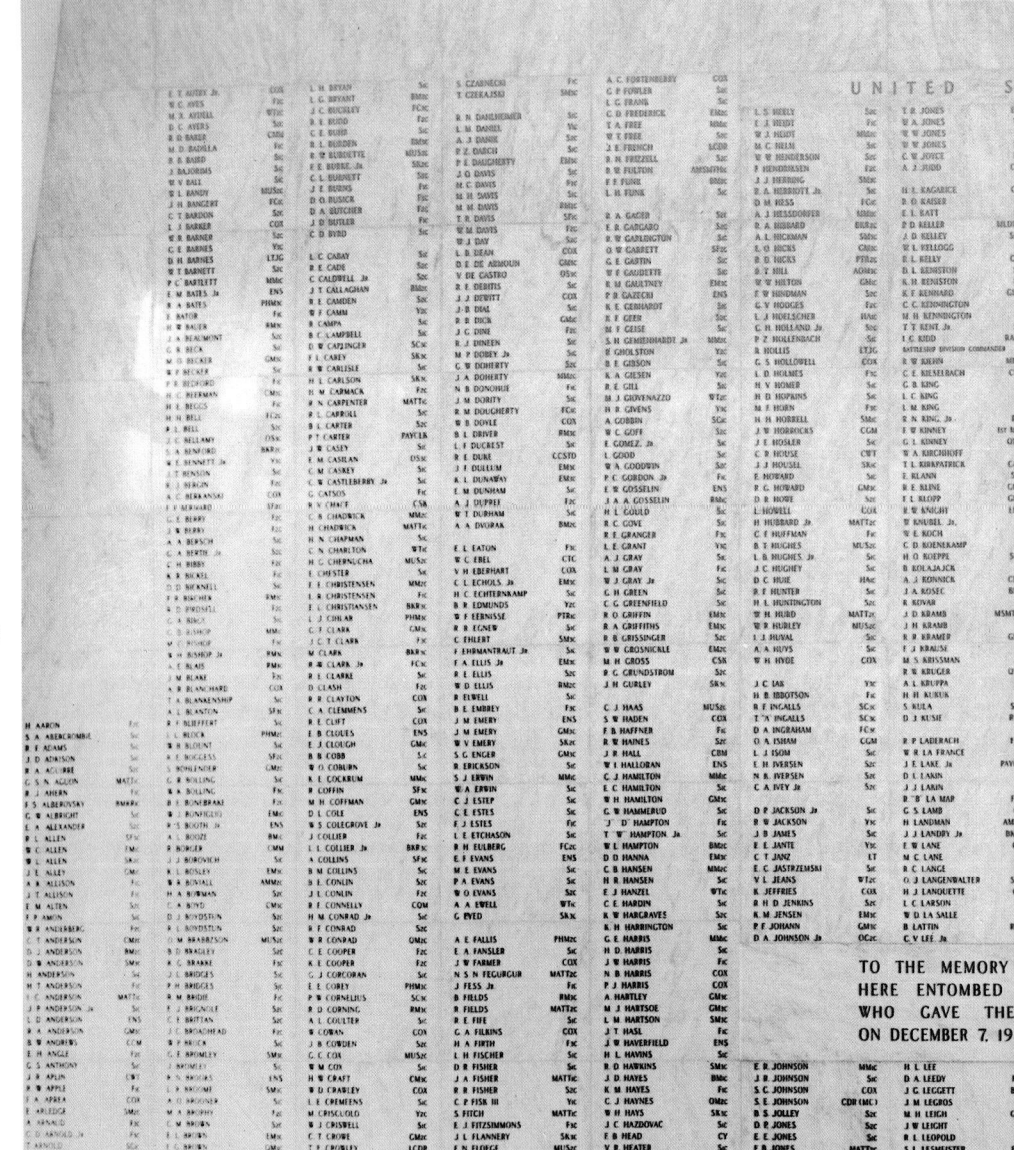

32

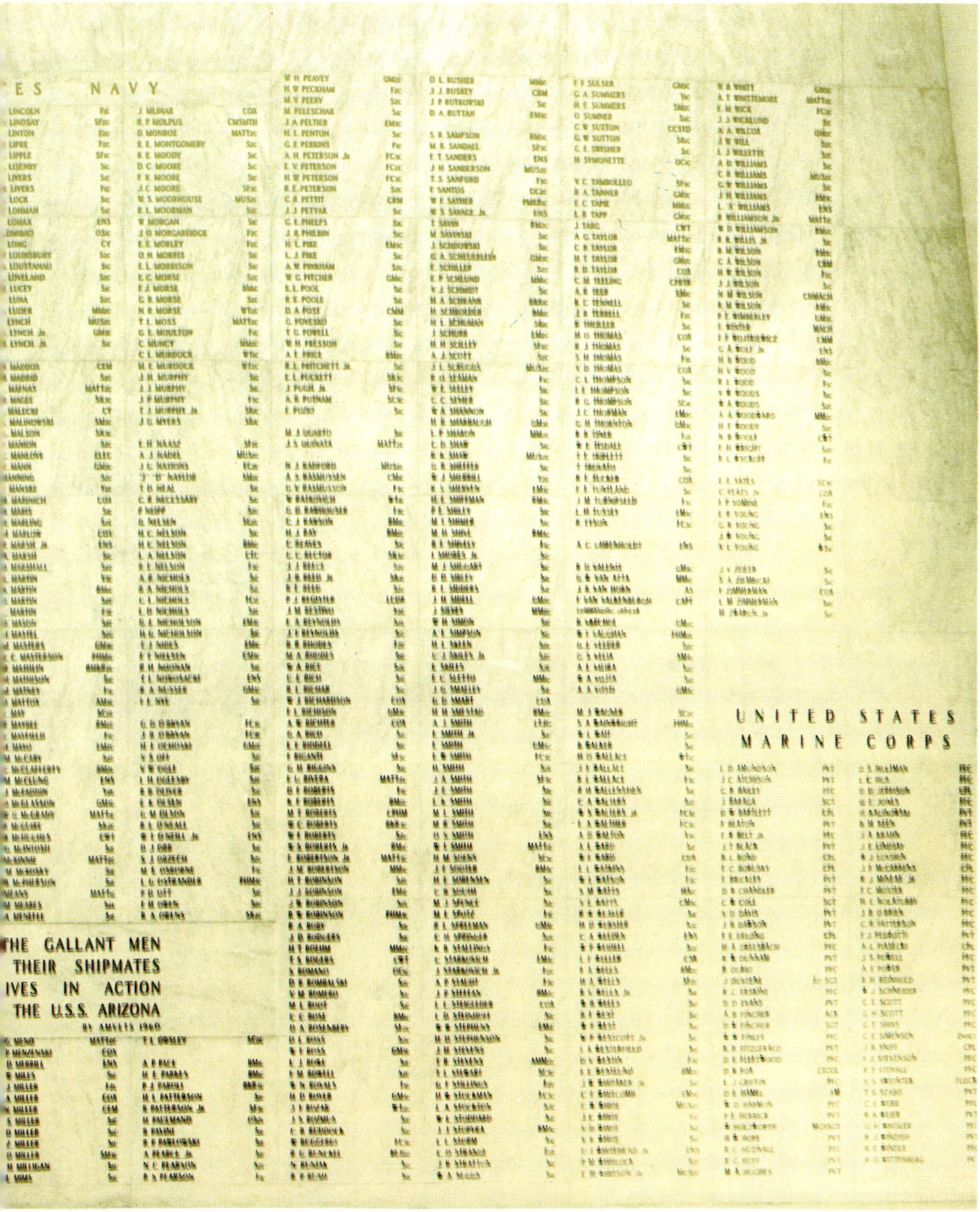

ES NAVY

UNITED STATES
MARINE CORPS

THE GALLANT MEN
THEIR SHIPMATES
IVES IN ACTION
THE U.S.S. ARIZONA

Each year, on the anniversary of the attack,
services honoring all those who died are held on
board the Arizona Memorial.

USS WEST VIRGINIA AND USS TENNESSEE

were at the quays just south of the ARIZONA on December 7, 1941. The WEST VIRGINIA was outboard of the TENNESSEE and six torpedoes and two bombs left her a flaming wreck. She settled to the bottom with her main deck awash. The Commanding Officer, Captain Mervin S. Bennion, was killed in the action. The Fletcher-class destroyer BENNION (DD-662) honored his name.

After being raised and repaired the "WEEVEE" went back into the war.

She spent 223 days in battle actions and took all comers to the finish.

The TENNESSEE was pinned to the mooring quays until the WEST VIRGINIA was moved. The TENNESSEE's damage from bombs was not too severe and she was not hit by torpedoes, being protected by the WEST VIRGINIA. A grave hazard to the TENNESSEE was burning oil on the water, but the Captain thwarted that by running the propellers ahead for 24 hours, without moving.

The TENNESSEE's guns fought back throughout the attack. Later she took part in the Iwo Jima and Okinawa campaigns.

USS okLAHOMA

USS OKLAHOMA was moored outboard protecting the MARYLAND from torpedoes. The MARYLAND's damage was the least of any of the eight battleships in the harbor on December 7th. She was in active service in less than three months.

Shortly after the first Japanese bomb exploded on Ford Island the OKLAHOMA was blasted by three torpedoes in rapid succession. There was no time to prevent her capsizing because of the rapid listing. She took two more torpedoes as she capsized.

Men were strafed as they climbed over the rolling ship which stopped when the masts hit the mud of the harbor bottom. All of this in less than 20 minutes.

The OKLAHOMA lost 415 men from the total complement of 1,354. Thirty-two men trapped inside were saved by heroic efforts of rescuers who cut through the upturned bottom. The rescue efforts by sailors and civilian workers from the shipyard started during the attack, as they worked amid searing oil fires and deadly explosions.

USS CALifORNIA

USS CALIFORNIA (foreground) has just been hit and is listing slightly. At the stern of the NEOSHO (background) is the upturned bottom of the OKLAHOMA.

The NEOSHO had just delivered 500,000 gallons of aviation gasoline to the Ford Island Naval Air Station and had that many more gallons on board. Disregarding the danger of the volatile cargo, her guns opened fire at 8.05 a.m. and are credited with shooting down one enemy plane.

The NEOSHO was the first ship underway. Her captain knew they were blocking the way of the MARYLAND and the OKLAHOMA and while under attack chopped the mooring lines and backed away from the pier. The NEOSHO barely cleared the OKLAHOMA which was just rolling over as she moved to a "safe place."

The NEOSHO was undamaged during the December 7th attack but only five months later she was sunk in the Coral Sea after being hit by seven bombs and one suicide plane.

GENERAL ALARM

was sounded on the CALIFORNIA at 8:00 a.m. the Sunday morning of December 7th. Personnel in the ship's flag communications station watched the first torpedo hit.

At 8:05 a.m. two explosions rocked the CALIFORNIA setting off an ammunition magazine and killing 50 men. The ship shuddered, rolled to an eight degree list and started to settle. The CALIFORNIA had been scheduled to undergo an inspection and watertight integrity was not at maximum, thus accounting for the immediate flooding.

Bomb hits now started fires, and burning oil in the water erupted into a blazing wall of fire surrounding the ship. "Abandon ship" was ordered. The men immediately started fighting the fires with equipment from Ford Island. Soon "abandon ship" was cancelled and the men returned. Despite valiant efforts to keep her afloat, the CALIFORNIA settled into the mud.

However the CALIFORNIA was raised and ready for battle in time for the capture of Saipan and Guam. She was active in all the island occupations up the line to Japan.

THE SECOND WAVE

of enemy planes met a concentrated screen of anti-aircraft fire as more ships' crews rallied and manned their guns.

Four cruisers were at the piers of the repair yard in Southeast Loch. The NEW ORLEANS and the SAN FRANCISCO were on opposite sides of one pier and the ST. LOUIS and HONOLULU were side by side at the next pier.

The SAN FRANCISCO's engines were under repair and her ammunition was ashore for safety. She went undamaged and cleared Pearl Harbor on December 16th.

The NEW ORLEANS was without power and could man only a few guns. She was ready to be underway December 23.

The HONOLULU had hull damage from a bomb that exploded under the pier but fired 7,750 rounds of ammunition. She went on duty January 2.

The ST. LOUIS' guns had to be operated manually but were credited with three probable "kills" during the attack of December 7th. At 9:31 a.m. she was underway and steamed out at 25 knots, the first big ship to reach open water.

USS OGLALA

USS OGLALA was outboard of the cruiser HELENA alongside "1010" dock. Normally that was where the battleship PENNSYLVANIA berthed and thus they became prime targets. Torpedoes were launched at the two ships by the first wave of attackers on December 7th. One torpedo passed under the OGLALA and exploded against the HELENA. The blast caved in the side of the OGLALA and she started flooding. Two commercial tugs were hailed. Working under constant danger, the tugs towed the OGLALA clear so HELENA could move out.

The OGLALA was secured to the dock, but capsized at 9:45 a.m. She was raised, rebuilt and supported the fighting ships through the war as a repair ship.

The HELENA went on her own power for overhaul. While in action in the South Pacific she was sunk by Japanese torpedoes off New Georgia on July 5, 1943. Of the 739 survivors, 165 spent 36 hours in the water and another 8 days on a jungle island before rescue.

THE BATTLESHIP PENNSYLVANIA

and the destroyers CASSIN and DOWNES were out of the water at Drydock No. 1.

The PENNSYLVANIA was not damaged seriously and soon was in action. She was Flagship on December 7th, but never again. On August 12, 1945, just two days before the war's end the PENNSYLVANIA was hit by a torpedo at Okinawa, the last major ship damaged in action.

The CASSIN and the DOWNES had raging fires under them from ignited fuel. The drydock was flooded to control the fires and the flooding caused the CASSIN to slip from her keel blocks and fall against the DOWNES. Both were thought to be lost.

The CASSIN was towed to San Francisco and rebuilt. She was to earn seven battle stars before the surrender of Japan.

All salvageable machinery and equipment of the DOWNES were shipped to Mare Island, and built into another hull. Her last duty was carrying homeward bound servicemen from Iwo Jima to California.

USS SHAW

suffered a devastating bomb hit which came late in the attack on December 7th. The detonation hit forward blowing up all the magazines and tearing off the entire bow. A deadly fountain of debris and shells ripped through the air, plummeting to the ground all around Pearl Harbor. The destroyer was in Floating Drydock No. 2. After the spectacular explosion the SHAW was reported sunk by Japanese flyers.

Pearl Harbor Shipyard workers fashioned a temporary bow, and with it the SHAW made a tedious voyage to San Francisco for permanent repairs. In July, 1942, she steamed out of the Golden Gate in her new battle dress. In October, less than one year after being a Pearl Harbor casualty, the ship was in action in the Solomons.

The SHAW was under attack in 11 battle actions winning stars for each engagement. Battle damage put her in drydock one more time and on V-J Day she was in San Francisco.

USS pHOENIX

USS PHOENIX steamed by the burning ARIZONA on her way to sea. Earlier, while moored in East Loch near the SOLACE, observers on the PHOENIX sighted the rising sun of Japan on the strange planes screaming in low over Ford Island. In the first minutes of the December 7th attack, PHOENIX gun crews fired on the attacking aircraft.

The PHOENIX was one of the ships unharmed during the disaster. Her escape was probably due to the attention enemy pilots paid to the capital ships in nearby "Battleship Row."

During 15 months in the forward fighting areas the cruiser earned 9 battle stars in 20 different actions. She is credited with shooting down eight torpedo or Kamikaze planes attacking her, and sinking a sub that had fired two torpedoes at her.

One enemy bomb burst in the water close to the PHOENIX wounding four men and killing one, the only man killed aboard the PHOENIX during the war. She well deserved the nickname "LUCKY PHOENIX."

ONE JAPANESE PLANE,

among those shot down, crashed in Honolulu. Japanese carriers dispatched 353 planes; 29 of them never returned. They were hit by anti-aircraft fire, or shot down in "dog fights" with Army planes. Enemy planes crashed all over Oahu, in Pearl Harbor, and in the ocean offshore. No serious damage to civilians or their property was reported from the crashes.

Strict blackout regulations and enforcement went into effect the night of December 7. Further enemy action was grimly anticipated. At 7:14 p.m., as Islanders sat tensely in their dark homes or in dark shelters, police radio announced that Pearl Harbor was being attacked again. There was an extravagant burst of fireworks over Pearl Harbor. Six planes from the aircraft carrier ENTERPRISE were coming in to land at Ford Island and, in a tragic instance of trigger-happy confusion, four of them were shot down. Sleep that night was scarce for both civilians and military personnel.

CIVILIAN CASUALTIES

included three Pearl Harbor employees on their way to their jobs. Sixty-five other civilians were killed elsewhere on the island; 50 or more were wounded seriously enough to require hospitalization; and more than 200 were less seriously wounded. Most of the casualties were on or near military bases, but some were in Manoa Valley, Downtown Honolulu, the Airport, Ewa and Waipahu.

The records of a Honolulu utilities office show more than 40 locations where bombs or shells impacted and were investigated. Twenty five of them caused damage to buildings and persons, 7 caused slight damage, 3 were followed by fires and 9 had no explosion or damage. Civilian damage on that day has been estimated at $500,000.

The opinion of experts is that most of the damage was a result of anti-aircraft fire from U.S. guns. Strafing near military bases and some bombs were definitely from the attackers, although their general plan obviously was to concentrate on military ships and airfields.

USS NEVADA

is shown leaving Pearl Harbor three months after the attack. The Japanese claimed they "destroyed to pieces" many ships that later showed up attacking them.

There were 94 vessels in the harbor at the time of the Japanese attack: 8 battleships, 9 cruisers, 31 destroyers, 5 submarines, and other auxillaries. By the end of the attack, about 9:45 a.m., 18 of them were damaged or sunk and couldn't get underway.

All but 3 of the 18 damaged ships were repaired and went into action in the weeks and months following the attack. The CASSIN and the DOWNES were rebuilt, and were never stricken from the active list.

Three were total losses. The OKLAHOMA was floated, sold for salvage and sank at sea while being towed to the West Coast.

The UTAH and the ARIZONA were left at their moorings and there remain to honor the men who gave their lives in action December 7, 1941.

PUNCHBOWL

is a flat topped hill only a short distance from downtown Honolulu. An extinct volcano crater estimated to be 75,000 years old, it's Hawaiian name is Puowaina, meaning reverence. Legend refers to the area as a resting place. In contrast to that peaceful image, guns were mounted on Punchbowl in the early days of the Monarchy due to its strategic position overlooking Honolulu Harbor.

In 1949 the 112 acres on the floor of the crater were dedicated as the National Memorial of the Pacific. More than 18,000 war casualties are buried here including veterans of the Spanish American War through the crisis in Viet Nam. Ernie Pyle, the well-known World War II correspondent, is among them.
The "Garden of the Missing" is a monument in Punchbowl dedicated to men missing in action. Its poignant inscription reads: "The Solemn Pride That Must Be Yours — To have Laid So Costly A Sacrifice On The Altar Of Freedom."

46

HONOLULU HARBOR

was under attack when the Dutch liner JAGERSFOUTEIN entered at 9:00 a.m. on December 7th. When bombs began to fall around them, the Dutch crew fired back and became the first ally to join our fight.

HONOLULU INTERNATIONAL AIRPORT

before commercial overseas flights were introduced, was a small landing strip and a few hangars known as John Rodgers Field.

A few private planes and instruction flights were out early on Sunday December 7, 1941. Just minutes before an inter-island flight to Maui was scheduled to take off at 8:00 a.m., catastrophe struck as Japanese attack planes began to strafe the airport, killing and wounding some of the civilians. The passengers were unloaded unharmed. The small planes in the air all managed to get back, though some were attacked and damaged by bullets.

GARDEN OF THE MISSING

Sincere appreciation is acknowledged to these individuals for their information or assistance in preparing this book.

Marion P. Goddard, Honolulu; Sara Jean Rice, Honolulu; J. A. Nowell, JO 2, Pearl Harbor; Captain G. T. Curren, USN (Ret.); Staff Sergeant Lee Embree, USAF; Grant Chapman; Staff of Bishop Museum Library, Honolulu; Staff of 14th Naval District Office of Public Information, Pearl Harbor; Staff of National Archives, General Services Administration, Washington, D. C.; Dale Nielson; Paul Jacobi; Phil Uhl; B. Dolman; Master Color Laboratories, Inc.; Staff of Tongg Publishing Co., Ltd.

PHOTO CREDITS

Official U. S. Navy Photograph: page 28, 32-33.

U. S. Office of War Information in National Archives: page 39.

U. S. Army Photograph: pages 1, 8, 9, 34.

Navy Department Photo in National Archives: pages 5, 6, 7, 12, 14, 15, 16, 17, 20, 21, 22, 23, 24, 25, 26, 27, 35, 36, 37, 38, 40, 41, 42, 44, 45.

Navy Department photo in National Archives with color by Rio Studios, N.Y.C.: Front cover and page 13.

Navy Department Photo with Pearl Harbor Film Service Color: page 2-3, 43.

Pearl Harbor Film Service: page 30 center.

SWAK, Inc. by W. T. Rice: pages 18-19, 30 upper and lower, 31, 46-47.
by Dale Nielson: page 29.
by Phil Uhl: back cover.